Life's Junctures & Sustaining Qualities

Exploring the Dynamism Inherent in One's Life Path & Attaining Equilibrium

By Michael Hooper

NEW FORUMS

NEW FORUMS PRESS INC.

Published in the United States of America
by New Forums Press, Inc.1018 S. Lewis St.
Stillwater, OK 74074
www.newforums.com

Copyright © 2019 by New Forums Press, Inc.

All rights reserved. No part of this publication may be reproduced or transmitted in any form or by any means, electronic or mechanical, including photocopy, or any information storage or retrieval system, without permission in writing from the publisher.

Library of Congress Cataloging-in-Publication Data Pending

This book may be ordered in bulk quantities at discount from New Forums Press, Inc., P.O. Box 876, Stillwater, OK 74076 [Federal I.D. No. 73 1123239]. Printed in the United States of America.

ISBN 10: 1-58107-335-6
ISBN 13: 978-1-58107-335-5

Contents

Foreword v

Chapter 1 – Introduction 1

Chapter 2 – Research Review 7

Chapter 3 – A Life Journey Case Study 15

    Growing Up in Pennsylvania 15

    Off to College in California 19

    "You're in the Army Now…..". 23

    From the Military to the Quasi-Military, LAPD 30

    Off to "Linebacker U"—Penn State 38

    Back to the "Left Coast" 40

    An Afterthought about Sustaining Qualities 42

Chapter 4 – Respondents' Selections of Sustaining Qualities 45

    Qualities Identified by Respondents 46

    Qualities Identified by Students 57

Chapter 5 – Epilogue 61

References 65

About the Author 67

Foreword

Michael Hooper and I have some things in common, the first being that we served together in the same rifle company – C Company, 1st Battalion, 52nd Infantry Regiment – in Vietnam in early 1970. Our paths re-intersected after almost 50 years at a reunion of the company's veterans in Saint Louis, MO.

Another thing we have in common is our conviction that our lives have been uniquely shaped through individuals we have encountered and interacted with over the years, along with key events we experienced. We realized this commonality after only briefly visiting during and after the reunion.

Also, we have in common our involvement in education, specifically higher education and what is termed "scholarly writing." Over the years, Mike progressed from a college student, to an infantryman, to law enforcement, to graduate school, and then to professor/scholarly writer. At the same time, I journeyed from a college student, to an infantryman, to a return to graduate school, to public relations, and finally to what is termed "scholarly publishing."

There are the unique intersections of our lives – infantrymen and scholarly writers/publishers. And, there is the unique purpose of this work – to emphasize the dynamism inherent in a life path and to identify key qualities that sustain a life journey, despite unanticipated intersections with people and events affecting life course changes.

In this title, Mike mines sustaining qualities from his own journey as well as from those who have impacted significantly his life path. And, hey, that includes me! Clearly, I highly recommend this novel work, especially to young people who are anticipating and entering their life's journey, in the hope they and others (you the reader) may glean the greatest possible benefit from your key qualities and the significant people and events you will encounter.

> Douglas O. Dollar, Ed.D.
> Maj. Gen., USA, retired
> President, New Forums Press

Chapter 1

Introduction

This guidebook's purpose is to emphasize the dynamism inherent in a life path and to identify key qualities that sustain one along a life's journey, despite unanticipated intersections with people and events that affect life course changes. The stimulus for initiating the book project came upon me unexpectedly. After earning a living for almost 50 years, I decided to embark on the life-changer known as "retirement." Surprisingly, something unanticipated occurred soon after taking the plunge: I found myself preoccupied with the question, "How in the world did I arrive at the place where I've found myself today?" Last time I attempted to formally chart an aspirational life path was in the mid-1960s. According to that initial chart, by now, decades later, I should have been looking back at an aviation-related career—not as it has evolved, i.e., a law enforcement practitioner and a university professor. Though, for reasons I will detail later, I am deeply grateful for the outcome realized. To have attained longevity in the practitioner and teaching professions has been extremely heartening. Early life circumstances were not conducive to attaining nearly such an outcome, nor was the untethered manner in which I traversed my life path.

This process of reflection was new for me as I had always found myself looking forward more than backward. Perhaps, it came with the realization that I indeed had actually crossed the finish line in a "race" undertaken five decades ago. I had finally reached the point where I no longer needed to perform the daily calculation of how much more workplace time investment was required to achieve the financial threshold needed for a livable retirement.

Interestingly, the reflection evolved to self-inquiry as to just what accounted for the departure from the envisioned future path, and, in consideration of the redirection, what were the qualities that in hindsight enabled and sustained me in the actual life path taken. I found that I carried the thought with me into the classroom where I continued in retirement in the same part-time teaching position held at a local university as when working full-time at the California Department of Justice. I now reviewed the students' career ambition cards completed at the beginning of each semester in a different light. Placing myself in their shoes as one poised to enter the fray of the workplace, I recognized that a good number of their enumerated career aspirations would likely not materialize with the specificity envisioned. Undoubtedly, unanticipated intersections with people and incidents would intervene to effect course changes. I pondered what would prove to be the prominent qualities that would sustain them in their endeavors to navigate a life's journey amid seemingly inevitable redirections.

With all due respect to "Forrest Gump," whose mythical life path I paralleled in a number of ways, I had found life to be much more like a pinball machine than a box of chocolates. Making a selection from a box of chocolates is a rather static process, and really the outcome can be somewhat predictable, i.e., soft creams are usually tear-dropped and caramels are square or rectangular in shape, etc. (factoid gleaned from way too much personal experimentation). In contrast, a pinball's journey is one fraught with dynamism and critical junctures, where the course taken is constantly shaped by the interplay of ball and "bumper" (a bumper being one of those electronically infused outcroppings the pinball bumps against and is instantly propelled asunder).

Metaphors aside, people often do seem to embark on their life journey anticipating predictability as a constant. More importantly, they frequently do not recognize the extent to which junctures, i.e., critical points in time resulting from a concurrence of circumstances, will quite likely intervene to promote decision making of lasting significance.

Given this post-retirement perspective, I became far more aware of the angst suffered by many young adults who believe they must lock in on a career path or a specific life track by the day of college graduation. For those not choosing to attend college, it is likely the same concern would surface as high school graduation draws near. Rather than merely "sit" on this recognition, i.e., that few of us ultimately find ourselves in the type work or the life track envisioned, I have sought to research and document the qualities that enable one to traverse a life path fraught with twists and turns and setbacks, and eventually arrive at a place of contentment—albeit likely not the destination originally planned.

The diagnostic process entails identifying the qualities that have in *hindsight* proved sustaining in my own life journey and, in turn, ascertaining from those individuals who have positively influenced my life path the qualities that have aided them in their own respective life journeys. The word "hindsight" is underscored in the preceding sentence to make clear that for much of my life I "flew blindly" in terms of knowing how to best navigate life. It is only through looking back in time with an accumulated breadth of insight that I have been able to deduce the actions and qualities that led to fruitful outcomes. At the time, I did not have the benefit of the guidance of a collective such as the one contributing to this retrospective study.

Admittedly, this quasi-transformation literary genre is altogether new to me. Heretofore, all my research and publications have involved criminal justice topics. I would like to note here at the outset that I had numerous gnawing concerns about what I was to undertake. A looming concern was my standing to inform others how to navigate life. But then I thought, "Well, who is better equipped than one who has bumbled along rather 'rudderlessly' to best appreciate the value of knowing, 'pre-journey,' the qualities that enable an efficient route of travel."

Following this credibility issue was the perception that writing about one's life experience can be an exercise in vanity. And for years I resisted family encouragement to write a memoir because I thought it to be precisely an exercise in vanity. But, then, I saw where benefit could accrue to those embarking on their life journeys. A related encouraging factor was to pay tribute to all those who played pivotal roles in positively influencing the direction of my journey. Thus, I wanted to offer up my life path for dissection, and to demonstrate one's life path is really a series of segments, each of which is an outgrowth of a key individual or event.

Of course, another concern was whether there would be a readership beyond the publisher's proofreader. In my survey of transformation- and memoir-type books in print, a recurring observation was that they either involved individuals who were wildly successful at accumulating wealth or involved people who had attained celebrity status. This realization was at first intimidating. After all, who would care about the travails of "Joe or Joy Ordinary?" However, at the same time, it revealed a lack of coverage of life paths of "ordinary" people—those of us who make up 95+ percent of the populace. Moreover, who can say that an ordinary person's life is really any less fraught with challenges and "hills to climb." Certainly, challenges are relative in terms of what it takes for an individual to achieve a satisfying outcome in any given endeavor. Ordinary life is heroic in its own way too, considering the extent to which the average person must perform to sustain a livelihood and a household, given finite resources. So, researching and passing along lessons learned by so-called ordinary people successfully traversing the pathways and junctures of a life journey clearly seemed to be the right thing to do.

Another issue was how to limit the scope of what would be detailed about my own life path. The scope needed to include the intersections with key events and figures. I decided to accentuate the positive aspects of junctures. After all, we are seeking the gold nuggets from experience and knowledge gained. The section (Chapter 3) is the lengthiest one in the book, but, then, it is the one place that illustrates the context of all individuals and events comprising significant junctures.

Too, concern arose regarding privacy, my own and that of contributors. Therefore, the names (last and/or first) of contributors have been changed to the extent needed to mask identities. Factual circumstances are detailed as they occurred.

The documentation process begins with a review of pertinent research findings, both those based on empirical evidence and those based on unverifiable, but compelling, beliefs. The review centers on factors that commonly influence an individual's life path and on methods for navigating amid the unforeseeable to attain best outcomes.

Next, I trace my own life path as a vehicle for identifying junctures, or bumpers, that have contributed significantly toward influencing my own life journey and for identifying the related sustaining qualities. While only a single life track, it has been one that has enabled insight into a wide array of human behaviors and related sustaining qualities. My service with the LAPD for more than two decades afforded enormous exposure—from "skid row" and its inhabitants to the multi-millionaires residing behind the exclusive Bel Air's gates. Too, being in the U.S. Army at the time of the draft—amid the Vietnam War—was an eye-opener into varying backgrounds and humankind under extreme stress. Teaching students over three decades has provided insights into a wide range of personality types, and in several cases I have been privy to their post-graduate lives. Too, there are contrasting lifestyles experienced through growing up in Pennsylvania's coal-mining region and attending college in sunny and vibrant southern California. The autobiographical life path sketch provides the context for identification of key sustaining qualities that emerged through my interactions with myriad others.

The process next gathers insights via self-report narratives from individuals I encountered who were influential along the course of my life path. Their own perceptions of sustaining qualities for achieving fulfilling outcomes are combined with mine. The pooled qualities are then quantified and ranked, yielding a composite of key sustaining qualities identified by an array of experienced individuals.

The process concludes by examining the mindsets of young adults just starting their life journeys. The population of college students comprising an introductory public policy course was queried as to what they believed to be key qualities that would sustain them in their quests toward realizing their career aspirations. Their prominent qualities are contrasted with those of the experienced life path travelers.

The intended takeaway for the readership is twofold: 1) reduction in the angst suffered among young adults overly concerned about specificity in workplace or life-track alignment, and 2) insight into sustaining qualities experienced by long-time life path travelers. Too, there is a takeaway for those of us who have been on life's journey for eons. We can retrace our past to ascertain junctures encountered and how we contended with them to arrive at where we find ourselves today, and how derivative qualities can lead to an optimal future state.

Chapter 2
Research Review

In this review of the applicable research, the focus is on the form and nature of junctures commonly experienced along life paths. In addition, the coverage includes best practices for realizing fruitful outcomes in the wake of junctures.

In terms of rigor, any review of the literature within the realm of life path determinants should commence with the scholarly contributions of Albert Bandura, widely described as the greatest living psychologist and one of the most influential of all time (Cherry, 2018, p. 2). Dr. Bandura advocated that chance encounters play a prominent role in shaping the course of human lives; some fortuitous encounters touch only lightly while others branch people into new trajectories of life. In Bandura's view, chance encounters affected life paths through reciprocal influence of personal and social factors. By this he meant that if persons are to reap the benefit of affiliation with whom their lives intersect there must be mutual emotional ties and shared values and standards. Similarly, individuals affiliate with groups when social rewards are high, and there is mutual affinity. Once attached, individuals are socialized into the group's ideology and lifestyle. Moreover, "chance encounters have the greatest potential for branching persons into new trajectories of life when they induct them into a relatively closed milieu," provided such is in a socially valued direction. In addition, Bandura emphasized beyond possessing effective interpersonal acumen, social supports are essential to surmount the obstacles and stresses encountered along life paths (Bandura, 1982, p. 754). Thus, conceding the unpredictability of chance encounters, Bandura did offer that the potential for favorable outcomes from such encounters can be increased when converging actors' personal proclivities and social factors are aligned.

Expanding on Bandura's research, the research team of Madelon Peters, Ida Flink, Katja Boersma, and Steven Linton (2010) demonstrated through 44 study participants that merely imagining a positive future can indeed induce optimism. The finding suggested that we can change both how we feel in the moment and how we feel about what is yet to come. Thus, by having had induced optimism, the prepared mind would be in an optimal state to use any chance encounter in the most positive way. Moreover, combining this with social supports also promotes resilience and perseverance.

In analyzing the results of the Peters et al. study in the context of fortuitous circumstances influencing one's wellbeing, Daniel Tomasulo emphasized the core challenge is to cultivate and retain as much optimism as can be mustered in anticipation of the unforeseen. Quoting Heraclitus, Dr. Tomasulo (2011, p. 3) offers, "If you do not expect the unexpected, you will not find it…"

Psychologist Richard Wiseman has spent his career studying the concept of "luck." In the case of chance opportunities, he has concluded that lucky people consistently encounter such opportunities, but unlucky people do not. Through a variety of experiments, Dr. Wiseman found that so-called lucky people generate their own good fortune through four basic principles. First, they are skilled at being well positioned to notice and avail themselves of chance opportunities. They do this in various ways, including networking and simply being open to new experiences. Second, they take steps, e.g., meditation, to enhance their intuition. Third, they create self-fulfilling prophecies through positive expectations. Finally, lucky people are characterized as adopting a resilient attitude. Lucky people tend to imagine spontaneously how any bad luck they encounter could have been worse. In turn, this mindset helps keep their expectations about the future high (Wiseman, 2003, p. 3).

The notion of a properly attuned mindsight overriding severe environmental or fate-based deficits has been illuminated convincingly through the pioneering efforts of psychologist Carol Dweck. Dr. Dweck has repeatedly demonstrated through numerous studies of both children and adults that a "growth mind-set" can enable individuals to face and overcome all manner of challenges. She has identified two core mindsets: a fixed mindset based on the premise that one's abilities were carved in stone, and a growth mindset based on the belief that one's skills could be cultivated through effort and perseverance. The key she found is not ability; it is whether you look at ability as something inherent that only needs to be demonstrated (albeit, without ongoing practice) or as something that can be developed (through effort and rigor) (Gross-Loh, 2016).

Victoria Rubin, Jacquelyn Burkell, and Anabel Quan-Haase (2011) explored serendipity in the context of everyday life by analyzing naturally occurring accounts of chance encounters in blogs. Their research resulted in creation of a conceptual framework on facets of serendipity in everyday chance encounters. Central to their model is the concept of the "find," or a person who is discovered to be useful in some way. The "find" becomes relevant to a person with a prepared mind and who also has the capacity to "notice." Fortuitous outcomes gained from serendipitous events rely critically on acute observation. The research suggested that individuals who have a general orientation toward acquiring information and whose demeanor is open and agreeable are more likely to notice "finds" or useful information incidentally.

In an analogous vein, Malcolm Gladwell has given substantial weight to individuals with particular sets of social gifts, i.e., "finds," for their ability to turn ideas into great successes ("epidemics" in Gladwell's slang). He describes these individuals as "connectors" (the social equivalent of a computer network hub), "mavens" (information specialists or brokers), and salesmen (accomplished negotiators) (Gladwell, 2000). Gladwell advocates exploring serendipitously a wide spectrum of concepts and filing them for potential future use, which may be exploited down the road through an encounter with an appropriate information broker (Carmichael, 2016).

One of the more intriguing chance occurrences involved the late Apple and Pixar CEO Steve Jobs (2005). Jobs famously recounted in his Stanford University commencement address how his incidental enrollment in a calligraphy class at Reed College—soon after dropping out as a full-time student—fortuitously yielded the beautiful typography characteristic of both Mac and Windows computers. Jobs had been struck with the exquisite quality of the calligraphy on the posters that adorned Reed College. He henceforth enrolled in the college's calligraphy class where he learned about what makes great typography superior. Ten years later when designing the first Macintosh computer, what he had learned in the class came back to him, and he designed it all into the Mac. Jobs noted that had he not dropped out, he would never have dropped in on the calligraphy class, and personal computers might not have the wonderful typography that they do. In hindsight, he appreciated that at the time of taking the calligraphy class it was impossible to appreciate its future application, i.e., to "connect the dots" looking forward. However, he reasoned that one has to trust that the "dots" will somehow connect in your future. From this he learned the importance of having to trust in something, whether it be one's gut, destiny, or life, or karma. Thus, from Albert Bandura and his academic colleagues to Steve Jobs—social scientists through the hard-nosed practitioner—unadulterated rigor yields what may account to some degree for successful outcomes in the wake of chance encounters: personal and social acumen, social supports, preparedness in conjunction with optimism, inquisitive mindset, openness, and trust.

Presently, material and spiritual views are divergent with regard to life path determinants and sustaining qualities. As pointed out by Jeffrey Mishlove (1997)—bearer of the only doctoral diploma in parapsychology to be awarded by an accredited American university (University of California, Berkeley)—in his seminal encyclopedia, *The Roots of Consciousness*, those subscribing to scientism as the hallmark of rational enlightenment view anyone attesting to phenomena such as telepathy, clairvoyance, or precognition as either suffering pitiable delusion or perpetrating contemptible fraud. However, as an objective researcher one cannot dismiss altogether citing forces or influences unverifiable by conventional scientific methods that qualified devotees would offer as contributing significantly to where an individual finds one's self along a particular life path.

Of course, too, there is the domain of religion, with its hallmark belief in a supreme being. One's faith is tied to a set of beliefs, and the measure of a religion is its best ideals. All religions try to raise the questions that matter the most. The array of such questions often includes, for example, "What is the meaning of life?" or "What is the nature of God?" For eons, people have looked to their religions for some sense of the whole picture of life and for guidance as to best paths to pursue amid myriad dilemmas common to the human condition. For those who have a faith-based relationship with God, prayer is a direct means for communication. How a circumstance conveyed through prayer plays out is ultimately in accordance with God's will. A devout individual might be predisposed to take any concern to God, trusting Him to work it out or care for her/him in some way (Adamson, 2000).

Carl Jung, the prominent Swiss psychiatrist and protégé of renowned physicist Wolfgang Pauli, coined the term "synchronicity" to describe what he believed to be a coincidence of events that seem to be meaningfully related (Surprise, 2012). Rodney and Janice Dietert (2014, pp. 158-159) have made the point that rather than attempting to decode what synchronicities might mean within the cosmos we should take advantage of their occurrence. They advocate actively seeking them and using synchronicities to gain better command over our interactions with the relevant informational patterns. In the spirit of Dr. Jung, if someone were thinking about taking a vacation to a location either drivable or flyable and a fly landed on the person's head while she was pondering the mode of transportation, Jung might claim that synchronicity indicated it would be best to fly to the destination. While synchronicity does have its staunch adherents, unfortunately there is not abundant empirical evidence to support its existence (Radford, 2014, p. 3).

Prominent clairvoyant Ellen Tadd (2017) impresses that the spirit, soul, and personality are integrated. According to Tadd, spirit is the God force that animates and suffuses everyone and everything. She believes that past lives provide the grounding for current experiences, including negativity (traceable to what Tadd terms "first errors"). By actualizing our spiritual nature, i.e., attuning our conscious mind with spirit, we can break the momentum of the karmic snowball." The essence of Tadd's guidance, as outlined in her handbook, *The Infinite View: A guidebook for Life on Earth*, is provision of tangible tools to better navigate the inevitable highs and lows life brings. Such tools include techniques such as "third-eye focus" to help perceive uncomfortable or challenging circumstances and to maximize the quality of response. It is interesting to note that while as unscientific as Tadd's concepts may appear to the scientific community, she did grow up within a household where the scientific method was emphasized by her scientist father. And she fully acknowledges that she too would have doubts were it not for the confirmation that has come from her personal metaphysical experiences, trusted others, and thousands of students trained to become sensitive to the reality of spirit.

While in the spirit of the influence of past lives on existing ones, any discussion of reincarnation as potentially impactful for one's life journey must be inclusive of the contribution of the spiritual philosophy of Edgar Cayce. Mark Thurston (2017) has had a unique opportunity to apply the materials from Cayce's archives toward examining the thesis that we each have a special set of attributes and a purpose in life that involves making a contribution to the greater good that no one else can do in quite the same way. The Cayce readings propose that each soul chooses just before birth a specific mission. Dr. Thurston distilled from Cayce's materials several exercises for self-identifying and validating an individual's purpose in life. Thurston's classic guide, *Discovering Your Soul's Pur-*

pose: Finding Your Path in Life, Work, and Personal Mission the Edgar Cayce Way, is replete with indicators for determining alignment with one's life purpose. Through recognition of the symptoms of misalignment, there is opportunity for selection of best choices when encountering junctures amid a life path.

In concluding the review of non-material resources, it is instructive to point out the extent of separation between traditional science and the spiritual realm has been narrowing. This has been illustrated, perhaps most convincingly, by Apollo 14 astronaut Edgar Mitchell's epiphany upon his trip back from the moon. He recollected feeling a profound sense of universal connectedness. In Dr. Mitchell's own words, "The presence of divinity became almost palpable." The experience led Mitchell to conclude that reality is far more complex than conventional science led him to believe. It was this intersection of knowledge that led Mitchell to launch the interdisciplinary field of noetic science (Institute of Noetic Sciences [IONS], 2018).

Chapter 3

A Life Journey Case Study

This chapter's purpose is two-fold. It is the vehicle for identifying junctures and sustaining qualities in my own life journey. More importantly, it enables a marked expansion of the array of sustaining qualities through identifying individuals, and their context in my journey, who have contributed their thoughts on prominent sustaining qualities. The next chapter details those other individuals' perspectives.

Growing Up in Pennsylvania

My life began with a bit of a bump. I underwent two major surgeries by the time I turned three. When I was four years old our family relocated from the cozy home my father, Harry, had built in urban central Pennsylvania to move in with my mother's (Anne's) father in the nearby countryside. He needed living assistance, but there was no consideration given to placing him in an assisted living facility (referred to disdainfully as a "nursing home" in those days). The property was located midway between a state mental hospital and a large cemetery—we often commented that we lived between insanity and death. Quite possibly, the hospitalizations and the move from the city to the country was foundational for development of *adaptability*.

I attended first through third grade in a one-room schoolhouse. Students took turns fetching wood and coal from an adjacent shed for heating and for warming water for washing hands. In hindsight, the one-room schoolhouse was a showcase for what could be accomplished with a bit of *resourcefulness*.

I attended fourth grade in a two-room schoolhouse—a step up. The next two years were spent at a brand new state-of-the art elementary school. At the time, I was a good student, both academically and behaviorally. In fact, I was given the privilege of using the school PA system to announce the arrival of the various buses at the end of the school day. I was also a regular cast member in school plays. Thus, the practice of *sociability* had yielded sizable benefit.

Near the end of my elementary school days, my parents divorced in the wake of my mother's leaving with another man for a preferred life in California. I was 10 years old, and my two at-home brothers, Pat and Tom, were 6 and 15, respectively. (Brother Dick was the oldest and was serving a three-year hitch in the Marines.) We were each given responsibility for household tasks, ranging from meal preparation to dishwashing, to exterior tasks such as taking out the trash and keeping the grass cut, shoveling snow, etc. Again, *adaptability* became a necessity.

Despite Harry's saintly commitment, the divorce had a huge impact. A nurturing environment and traditional child care had for the most part evaporated. After all, how much could be expected of a single parent having to perform his trade as a carpenter from sun up to sundown and then go bill collecting and responding to estimates for potential next jobs in the evenings and on weekends. Further compounding matters, in the course of the divorce proceedings, my father became liable for a significant amount of money in order for us to continue to reside on our property. The fiscal situation at home was bleak.

At the beginning of each school year, we would get a couple pair of pants, some shirts, some socks, and a pair of leather shoes. We had a shoe stretcher device that enabled us to make the shoes a size or so larger as the year wore on. This attire would pretty much last us through the year. The dismal financial situation did introduce the concept of prioritization; at the time, it was more important to have clothes than preventive dental and medical treatment.

Involvement in neighborhood sports was extraordinary. My

brother Pat and our neighborhood buddies played the big three sports (baseball, basketball, and football) with great passion. School studies became secondary to sandlot sports. The parents of our neighborhood chums must be commended for their tolerance. My brother and I were unrelenting in our recruiting appearances at our buddies' doorsteps and undoubtedly pre-empting the day's plans parents might have had for their children. If nothing else, our efforts were illustrative of seizing the *initiative*.

We built our own sports venues. A baseball backstop was constructed from building materials that our father had left over from jobs. We borrowed a neighbor's tractor to sculpt the baseball field. When autumn rolled around, we built goal posts from swing sets, which we hauled onto the field to convert it for football. Basketball was played on the driveway, and we fashioned a backboard from wood scraps, and a peach basket (in the tradition of the sport's founder, James Naismith) served as a hoop. Later, I made a metal rim at school. The basketball court grew in size as batches of concrete left over from our father's construction jobs enabled driveway expansion. I had a newspaper route, and the route's profits were used to purchase bats, balls, and other sports incidentals. Additional revenue was brought in through picking cherries and raspberries and selling them along the road. Once again, *resourcefulness* came to the rescue.

When possible, we engaged other neighborhoods in a few games. These frequently ended with our gang on the wrong end of massacres. Involvement in the array of sporting endeavors was a product of *resourcefulness, initiative,* and *networking*. In addition, the fact is that we were solely responsible for all the logistics. Perhaps, more significantly, we self-resolved any and all disputes among ourselves, opponents, or neighbors—a practice that decades later would be formalized publicly as "restorative justice." This self-reliance was an outgrowth of *initiative, resourcefulness*, and *adaptability*.

For me, school work was a distant second to preoccupation

with "sandlot" sports. At the same time, I was emotionally and socially immature. My somewhat self-initiated migration away from the school milieu evolved—or, rather, devolved—to shortsightedness. The long-term benefit to engagement in scholastic endeavors and social activities was not apparent. Therefore, I did not give attention to enrolling in the kind of coursework or extracurricular activities that would enhance chances for college acceptance. I went into "drift" mode, merely acquiescing to what seemed would be the minimal effort to advance to the next grade level.

This immaturity was aggravated by the poor condition of my teeth. This dental deficiency, along with the lack of an adequate wardrobe and a skinny physique, made for a socially awkward demeanor. Thus, I further withdrew into the neighborhood sports scene, where I received a satisfying degree of respect from others and self.

Graduation from high school was accompanied by a decision to take some stop-gap action about the terrible condition of my teeth—a burst of *initiative* and a spark toward *sociability*. I found a humanitarian dentist who agreed to perform restorative work for a nominal fee.

Coincidental with getting my teeth restored to a semblance of what they were pre-decayed, I had begun to consider rejoining society at large. Around the same time, my brother Tom married a young woman, Jane, who added a softer side to the home environment (Jane and brother Tom lived in our household until they built their own on property to the rear of our home). Jane had been part of the social fabric of the community within which our junior and senior high schools were located. In this capacity, she represented the social strata that I had believed I was not a part of. However, Jane did in fact treat me as an equal socially, and this further encouraged *sociability*.

After graduating from high school, I assisted my father in his carpentry trade. As the fall evolved to winter, I became abundantly aware that I had no next step planned—and I recognized the construction industry was not my future. While I did not know what specifically interested me, I knew what did not. Through television and an occasional movie, I had glimpses of what other life formats existed and how—maybe, through extreme diligence—I could transform completely. This was the onset of mental preparation for mustering boundless *energy* and *perseverance*.

Given my lackluster resume to date, I felt that a new venue—a new start—might be what would be needed to begin to effect a makeover. Possibly, a college education would be the path toward rebounding and getting back into the mainstream and all it offered.

I had heard that California had an exceptional community college program with reasonable tuition and minimal entry requirements. California was also a land of abundant opportunity—unlike central Pennsylvania in the mid-1960s. My oldest brother had settled in southern California following his stint in the Marine Corps and was doing very well in the mortgage banking business following enrollment in a community college program. Also, my mother had remarried and was encouraging me to come to California. She was an apartment building manager and said that I could stay in vacant units or sleep on the sofa bed in her unit.

Off to College in California

Thus, given that I had very limited opportunities in Pennsylvania, with my father's blessings I decided to head to California. *Initiative* was thus undertaken on a grand scale, geographically speaking. I packed a couple suitcases to the brim with clothes and made flight reservations. I was also sure to include my "digging shoes," as I planned on earning money performing construction-related labor. "Nose to the grindstone" would be the mantra, and boundless *energy*—or *indefatigability*—the quality to be personified.

I boarded a flight to Los Angeles at Pittsburgh airport in August 1964. It was the first time I had been in an airplane and was captivated by the entire experience. The ambience of the cabin's interior appointments as well as the polish and poise of the flight crew made an indelible impression. It struck me that I had been introduced to a future lifestyle that at one time had been in reach, but through life circumstances and my own confusion and immaturity had almost been forfeited. I resolved while on the flight to expend whatever energy it took to regain control of my life and attain quality of life on all important fronts: family, workplace, and society.

Upon landing at "LAX," I was met by my mother (who I hadn't seen since she left Pennsylvania in 1956) and her husband, and my brother, Richard, and his gracious wife, Leigh. Richard was now a mortgage banker and Leigh was a full-time mom for three young girls.

College enrollment came around very soon. After registering, I made a beeline to the college's employment services office. There I had the good fortune of interacting with a kindly lady, Nan Goode, who seemed to take a maternal interest in my welfare. Nan sent my way several part-time jobs doing yardwork and odd jobs. While I had no prior gardening experience, the majority of people who placed the ads were knowledgeable about gardening, but preferred to have assistance with maintaining their yards. Under the tutelage of my "clients," I learned the basics of gardening and lawn care. *Adaptability* proved to be invaluable.

I soon developed a weekly gardening service for enough clients, thanks to Nan's referrals, to pay my bills. The pay was low but I could work the hours around my coursework, and some of the people treated me exceptionally well. Two of my gardening customers, Molly Strong and Marv Bilder, were exemplary in this regard. They were 100 percent supportive and always allowed college attendance hours to take precedence over when yard work would be completed.

Once the routine of work and college was set, I made a visit to the Santa Monica airport and inquired about flight lessons. The exuberant feeling I experienced from that cross-country flight of a few months ago had stayed with me. I learned that the cost of an hour lesson with an instructor was equivalent to a full day's yardwork wages. Obtaining a private pilot's license required a minimum of 40 hours flight time. I decided to go for it! I would pay as I go.

The flight training was not without its ups and downs (literally and figuratively), though. Midway through the training, I was required to make a cross-country solo flight. On the day of the flight, the skies were cloudy with intermittent rain along the flight path. The perils of flying in inclement weather as a novice were soon staring me in the windshield. The cloud cover had fully obscured the mountains. At this point in my flight training I had very minimal experience flying in clouds—and zero competency. I eventually made it to an airport south of the planned destination. Upon landing, I phoned my home base and told them where I was and was told to remain there, and a couple experienced pilots would come up to fly me back. During the flight back, my flight instructor said permission should never have been given for the flight, given the extreme weather conditions. I learned from this misadventure, in the spirit of "what doesn't kill you makes you stronger." While I would like to attribute some innate quality to surviving this potentially ill-fated flight, dumb luck—or some other-worldly power—was at play here.

After pulling mountains of weeds and doing any other odd job that was posted on the employment services board, I managed to make it through the requisite repertoire of flight maneuvers. By mid-1965, I was a licensed private pilot.

When calculating how much flight time would be needed for the commercial license (at least triple the amount of hours amassed to date), it became obvious that I needed to add to my work schedule. I retained the gardening customers, and let them know I was available to take on additional projects. Molly came through in a big way, both through referring me to the owners of the ranch where her family boarded their horses and referring me to other friends of hers. I spent substantial hours working at the ranch. Marv was also invaluable as he afforded opportunities to assist in his profession as a building contractor. This is where *relationship-building, networking,* and *indefatigability* melded as sustaining factors.

My younger brother Pat came to California in 1966, and we roomed together in an apartment building in the San Fernando Valley. In the next couple years, my older brother, Tom (and his wife, Jane) had relocated to California by now as well. Having both brothers close by, rather than way across the country, added a comforting measure of support.

By November of 1968 I was poised to graduate from San Fernando Valley State College (later renamed California State University, Northridge) and to complete the commercial pilot training program. Oh, but, too, there was one last remaining commitment that had to be addressed: military service. I had been given student deferments by my draft board all through college, and mine was to expire in January 1969.

As it turned out, only one of the two long-term goals would be completed without angst, which was the certification as a commercial pilot. The check ride by the FAA examiner went well, and I was now in possession of a significant flight certification—and the ability to charge for any flight services.

The goal of college graduation was fully on course in terms of what was expected of me. However, this was the era of student protests, and my college (in the seemingly sleepy San Fernando Valley) had gained the status of "hotbed of radical youth," as proclaimed by the *Los Angeles Times* (Clancy, 1985). The turbulent times included almost daily demonstrations over civil rights and the war in Vietnam. On one occasion in November, students took over the administration building. All this turmoil resulted in the campus being closed off and on, and my January graduation placed in jeopardy.

Compounding the angst, in mid-December my brothers and I received the crushing news that our father had suffered a fatal heart attack. He was only 57 years old. So, two brothers and I (my oldest brother remained in California but generously paid our air fares) flew back to Pennsylvania for the service.

As it turned out, final exams were not postponed and graduation did take place as scheduled in January 1969. Next order of business now was to pursue my military obligation. I spoke with a U.S. Army recruiter who informed me of a two-year enlistment option for college graduates. This was better than waiting to be drafted in that a reporting date would be known in advance. The enlistment entailed placement into an officer candidate pool, with the choice of attending or opting out of officer candidate school. I said, "Fine, sign me up." I left with a commitment to military infantry service on February 26, 1969.

Before entering the military in late February, I took an automobile trip to Las Vegas with my brothers Pat and Tom, Tom's wife, Jane, and her legal secretary friend from work, Joan England, who struck me as exemplary—and who unbeknownst at the time would in the next year prove crucial in my future life course in an unanticipated context. It was a whirlwind trip, but a very nice one.

"You're in the Army Now….."

Induction into the U.S. Army began early in the morning of February 26, 1969, at the Los Angeles induction center. After a long bus ride up the coast, we inductees arrived late at night at Fort Ord and were "welcomed" to our new home. We were led to a wooden barracks building, World War II vintage, I think, and bedded down for the night. Within a couple days we were assigned to another barracks, which would be home for the next eight weeks.

After graduation from eight weeks of basic training, I was assigned to an additional eight weeks of advanced infantry training (AIT), also at Fort Ord. Following completion of AIT in early July 1969, I was given leave of a few weeks or so before my next duty station, which would be Fort Benning, Georgia, for OCS. I spent the leave time with family in southern California and with Joan, with whom a close friendship had developed following letter writing while at Fort Ord.

As I progressed through the midway point of the 23-week OCS program, I increasingly gave thought to the fact that already I was one-third of the way through an original 24-month military obligation. If I remained on course for the remaining 23 weeks, I would be commissioned in February 1970 and then required to re-enlist for an additional three years. Discharge from the military under such circumstances would occur in February 1973. Alternatively, I would be discharged two years earlier, February 1971, if I exercised the option of pulling out of officer candidate school. I added to the mix for decision making the fact that military pilots would likely be entering the competition for airline jobs in increasing numbers as the Vietnam War was supposedly winding down. I mulled over the decision for a few weeks and largely in consideration of the envisioned career path in aviation, the elapsing time clock became of the essence. Thus, in the 15th week I withdrew from the program. This was the week before "ranger week," and because I was a non-swimmer thought it prudent to pull out before having to take a plunge into the Chattahoochee River from 40 feet above (part of ranger week exercises). *Prioritization* won out.

Orders assigning me to Fort Lewis, Washington, for overseas duty in Vietnam were soon in hand. In-processing at Fort Lewis began with a mandatory haircut, followed by issuance of jungle fatigues and boots. I was soon booked onto chartered Seaboard World Airways flight GD3V, leaving from McChord Air Force Base. After several hours, Cam Ranh Bay in Vietnam appeared through the airliner's windows. As we landed we were informed by the flight attendants of the temperature and given the customary spiel, "We enjoyed serving you aboard Seaboard World Airways and look forward to serving you on your return flight home." Possibly, this matter-of-fact approach was done for the mental health of the crew. I do not think it had any positive effect on us, though.

We were then loaded onto screened buses for delivery to the in-processing center. At our destination, paperwork was completed and we exchanged our U.S. currency for military payment certificates. Much later that evening (actually, closer to 3:00 a.m.) we were flown north to Chu Lai aboard C-130 aircraft. We then trucked to the Americal Division (23rd Infantry) headquarters for a week of Vietnam-specific combat training.

Upon completion of the week's training, I was assigned to

Charlie Company. Charlie Company was rather storied. Its reputation as a formidable fighting force was reinforced by the fact it was subsequently learned to be the most decorated company in the Americal Division from March through October 1970 (Buncombe County Veterans Council [BCVC], 2007). This was *service orientation* to the maximum. The unit, except for a few individuals assigned to administrative duties, was currently deployed in the field, a helicopter's ride away.

The next morning I went down to the rear area chopper pad at LZ Saber and waited for my lift to the "bush" to link up with Charlie Company. I had been given 10 meals of C-rations and instructed to take the first "bird" to "OP Mike." I boarded the chopper with two other "FNGs" (initials for a disparaging term, i.e., "f_ _ _ing new guys," reserved for new arrivals who potentially could jeopardize the lives of the experienced infantrymen). We soon landed at a makeshift landing area adjacent to a village that was being ringed by Charlie Company troops in anticipation of a possible Viet Cong offensive action.

The three of us walked through the village and reported to the location on the perimeter where the company commander was positioned within the Charlie Company command post. The command post consisted of the commanding officer, his RTOs (radio-telephone operators), an artillery forward observer, and his two assistants, a demolition man, Kit Carson Scouts (defectors who were formerly Viet Cong or NVA and now worked for the U.S. Army as scouts), and anyone else temporarily assigned to the company, e.g., dog handlers. My two chopper mates were assigned to line platoons, while I was told to remain at the command post (CP) for assignment as an RTO-in-training for the commanding officer, Captain Art Companico. Apparently, both individuals already serving as RTOs were getting "short," and their rotation out of the country was drawing close. *Adaptability* was essential both for me and for the good of the collective.

I soon became the primary RTO and as such carried the PRC 77 radio, which was the only radio that had the capability of sending secure transmissions. Each night we would hook it up to a scrambler unit, which was about the size of the radio and carried by another soldier, so that tactical and logistical information being transmitted to the tactical operations center would not be intercepted. For me, while having to tote a good-sized load with the radio, batteries, ammunition, regular and smoke grenades, the RTO position proved to be up my alley. I appreciated the opportunity to be working alongside the company commander and the responsibility for coordinating gunship support and medevacs, as well as helicopter resupply operations. Too, I was able to contribute to the safety of our personnel by responding at all hours to inquiries regarding locations where troops were deployed, e.g., as listening posts, observation posts, or ambush patrols in order to prevent harm from incoming artillery fire missions and air strikes. *Service* in this capacity was quite fulfilling.

Many have written about the military experience in Vietnam, and there have been numerous movies depicting it. I like to believe that I had no preconceived notions, despite having graduated from a somewhat liberal college, the student body of which as a collective likely opposed U.S. involvement. My philosophy teacher had said that Vietnam was about the United States' protecting its interest in tungsten, tin, and rubber resources. On the other hand, a widely held justification for U.S. involvement was the domino theory, i.e., stopping the spread of communism.

My first impression was, wait a minute, these guys who are doing the ground fighting don't look like stereotypical warriors. Most are pretty worn looking, not especially muscular nor very old at all—nothing like the Hollywood stars who have portrayed them on-screen. These are just guys off the street—many of whom have been drafted—who have been given 16 weeks of military training and sent off to engage an enemy bearing little resemblance to themselves either physically or culturally. Kudos for their collective *adaptability and commitment to service*!

Of course, the mission at hand was to locate and engage the

enemy. It was virtually inevitable that if there were to be substantial infliction of loss of life to the enemy, there would be some loss of life of U.S. "grunts." For the time period I served in Vietnam, from mid-January to late May 1970, 11 members of Charlie Company and a helicopter pilot made the ultimate sacrifice. Sadly, the two soldiers I helicoptered into Charlie Company with, became victims of fatal small arms fire.

One of our medics, "Rocky" Lente, represented the commitment to *service* by each member of the Charlie Company collective. "Rocky" was a draftee (as were the majority of Charlie Company personnel) from the San Francisco area who was also a conscientious objector. He represented well the liberal complexion of his hometown, with 1960s' iconography (a peace sign and the notation "War is not healthy for children and other living things") emblazoned on the rear of his flak jacket and multi-colored hippie beads around his neck (Crucq, 2017). In mid-April, his underlying valor and strength of character were on full display. On April 15 as our company was leaving a day laager en route to a place called Happy Valley, he was hit by small arms fire in the chest and right arm. Incredibly, he rolled over and dressed his own life-endangering wounds, not wanting to expose other medics to the continuing raking gunfire. Certainly, *initiative, perseverance*, and *service* commitment were full on. Compounding matters was the fact that when eventually he was aboard the medevac helicopter, he was shot again while in flight in the left and right arms.

My own wounding occurred on May 24, 1970, when a helicopter scout unit mistook our company as an enemy force. (There is an astounding form of synchronicity around this event that will be recounted later in the next section of this life path chronology.) As was a practice of scout choppers to draw return fire from an enemy position, the machine gunner aboard sprayed the area with gunfire. One of his bullets struck me in the left side of my upper back/lower neck. Another bullet struck a buddy in the hand. The gunfire rendered my radio inoperative. Fortunately, some clear thinker—obviously someone endowed with the *resourcefulness* "gene"—then popped smoke grenades, signaling to the helicopter the presence of "friendlies." Had the smoke grenades not been deployed, our company could have been decimated as the scout chopper had been assigned to adjust artillery fire on any potential enemy targets.

Following medical evacuation to the 27th Surgical Hospital in Chu Lai, I underwent surgery. After a second surgery in Japan, I was flown to Travis Air Force Base near Sacramento, California, and then on to Fort Ord for convalescence. I used the down time in the hospital to document my recollections of the time in Vietnam. In looking back on the war experience, the words of Colonel Gary Cassidy (2016, p. vii), author of a trilogy on his wartime experiences in Vietnam, ring insightful: "What a little responsibility and a few life-threatening situations will do for a young man on his road to maturity!" At that time in 1970 I was not really aware of the maturation that had occurred, but was very much aware of the extent to which I had been incredibly lucky and blessed.

Coincidental with being discharged from the hospital in August and returned to full duty, I became aware of the fact that the airlines were not in hiring mode. Matters had changed dramatically with the airlines as returning military pilots were gobbling up the jobs. And, too, the military pilots were far more qualified in terms of flight hours and jet experience than I. Thus, I became *vigilant* for other jobs.

I learned the Los Angeles Police Department was hiring. Perhaps, I could work for the LAPD until airline positions materialized again. I followed up with this lead, and an interview soon followed. I next met with a veteran police officer who would be conducting my background investigation, the make-or-break part of the selection process. He advised the listing of personal references, which excluded relatives, should be well-considered, and offered criteria which translated to a mix of impressive, high integrity individuals (male and female, peers and employers, etc.). Joan occupied the first position on the list of references, followed by one of my flight instructors, and then reputable professionals I had as gardening clients. This vetting would prove to be hugely pivotal, setting the stage for so much that would follow. In terms of sustaining qualities, the confluence of *sociability*, *relationship-building*, and *service orientation* had proved crucial. As will be evident later, entrance into the LAPD was a watershed event facilitated by key junctures and also enabling a succession of junctures culminating in family development, fulfillment in the workplace, and postgraduate education.

While I thought my chances for making it past my mid-20s had increased significantly since getting out of Vietnam, down the road—literally—there would be another too-close call. One early October weekend, I took a trip to the Lake Tahoe region from Fort Ord in my newly acquired Volkswagen "bug." The round-trip excursion took longer than expected. In hindsight I should have planned on lodging the night in Tahoe, but I pushed on, wanting to save money. As it turned out, the driving had made me weary beyond my self-awareness. Rounding a turn on highway 99 near Modesto, the right front wheel ran onto the shoulder, and when I corrected to the left the car skidded and rolled over. There I was, careening down highway 99 at about 2:00 a.m. or so, upside down. When the car finally came to rest in the middle of the roadway, still upside down, my impulse was to get out quickly, as I feared being struck by another vehicle. Something told me to push with my feet against the windshield, which popped out astonishingly easily. In a matter of seconds, I had crawled out and made my way well off the roadway. I came through the accident with just minor bruises and scrapes. Someone must have been looking out for me. I must say that I was concerned how the traffic accident might appear to the background investigators. Police departments had concerns about a candidate's driving record (and, too, I had received a citation for speeding prior to shipping out to Vietnam). The lesson learned in this instance was that the qualities of *initiative* and boundless *energy* can on occasion benefit from being "dialed back a notch."

From the Military to the Quasi-Military, LAPD

The police selection process was not without a couple hitches. For one, my medical records evidencing the origin of the gunshot wound (which had shown up on the physical exam) were not retrievable at the warehouse in St. Louis. Eventually, somehow that matter was resolved. However, when I was informed by the police department of an academy start date of November 30, and the military paperwork came through for my discharge—pursuant to a 90-day early out provision to join a law enforcement department—my serial number contained a typographical error. This snafu potentially placed in jeopardy the ability to start the academy session as scheduled. Moving more expeditiously than expected, the Army came through with the corrected copy of discharge orders—whew! Another of those sources of angst that would in few years manifest as ulcerative colitis.

At a very early time on the morning of November 30 (1970), I, along with 81 other hopefuls, reported for training at the LAPD training facility. This was not altogether different from in-processing for the military. We had drill instructors (predominantly former Marines) assigned to each squad (consisting of about 10 recruits). From day one, however, the training experience was more closely supervised than in the military, especially in the areas of physical training and gunnery techniques. There were more than 30 topics of instruction, and legalities were emphasized. A minimum of two hours daily were spent on physical fitness and self-defense tactics.

Speaking of physical conditioning, it seemed as if our class was exposed to overkill in the running aspect of conditioning. Many years later I learned that this was not a figment of my imagination. One of my academy classmates, Pat Gallup, confided that he had been a reserve officer prior to joining the police department as a full-time officer. He had known the physical training (PT) staff well as he was their running coach for a number of years. Pat confessed the PT staff "exploited" our class in that they gained their daily long distance running conditioning through running with us each day. Thus, our daily run at the end of calisthenics and self-defense tactics practice was likely twice the distance it would have been had the PT staff not been in long distance training mode.

The days and weeks passed slowly, but eventually April 16 arrived and with it graduation for 56 of us remaining from the original 82. *Adaptability* had facilitated graduation. Interestingly, one of my academy classmates was a furloughed Western Airlines pilot. It made me feel that I was in a pretty good place if even a pilot of his caliber was not able to retain a position with a commercial airline.

I was assigned to Central Area, which encompassed downtown Los Angeles. The precinct station was housed within the LAPD headquarters building. After completing the required probationary period, I was given a variety of patrol assignments, including the "drunk wagon" in "skid row" and both foot beat and automobile patrol. The foot beat and automobile patrol covered all portions of Central Area, which actually represented a microcosm of Los Angeles—except for the ocean component. I must say, too, that the cuisine ranged the gamut as well—all good: Mexican, Italian, hamburger joints, and steak houses. Life was good being a member of the LAPD and off probationary status.

All types of functions were housed within Parker Center. In support of major crime investigations, an auditorium within Parker Center served as the site for line-ups for suspect identification. One night in October 1971 a pretty and stylish young lady, Jill Beam, from the San Fernando Valley had come to the headquarters building to identify the suspect who had held her up at her bank workplace in the Valley. As I was assigned to work the front desk this particular evening and thus was effectively a host for individuals frequenting the building, I greeted Jill and inquired as to the circumstances of the robbery and the location of the bank in the Valley. It turned out her bank was just minutes from where I had an apartment in Studio City. Upon learning this, I said that I should open an account at the bank. Soon thereafter I followed through. Opening of a savings account evolved to a social relationship. *Initiative* and *sociability* proved fortuitous.

The department's position control office was located in Parker Center, and thus I was able to mosey up five floors and gain familiarity with job opportunities. As it turned out, I learned that a national police task force was at the moment looking for a research assistant to assist in the editing of a compilation of standards for policing, under the auspices of the National Advisory Commission on Criminal Justice Standards and Goals. I contacted the hiring authority and was given an interview and a grammar test. I was subsequently informed by my interviewer, Sergeant Chad Writer, that I had been selected for the position and I would be loaned from Central Area to the task force in the next few days. *Vigilance* opened the door to what would prove to be a whole other realm.

In my case, Chad proved to be a gatekeeper for entry into the world of staff work within the police department. I had no idea as to the quality of the position I had obtained through happenstance. Chad was a "bright star" within the department. He was valued in many ways by the top brass, and receiving a very favorable personnel rating report from Chad constituted a seal of approval for the ability to perform completed staff work, not only at the department level but at a national government level as well. The exercise of *initiative* had reaped a huge career benefit.

Coincidental with my loan to the task force, I embarked on a dental restorative process. I had pledged to myself that as soon as I landed a job that would yield sufficient income to enable restoration of my teeth, I would go for it without hesitation. I had been referred by one of my closest former gardening customers to a dentist renown as spectacular by his peers. *Networking* and *perseverance* thus culminated in a crowning achievement.

Shortly after returning to patrol work, I *initiated* a *vigilance* posture and went on the lookout for a permanent staff position. With my recent evaluation report in hand, I interviewed for an advertised position in the Public Affairs Division. I got the job, which entailed coordinating special police-community events. A big plus to the position was the camaraderie with my fellow workers, all young officers getting their first taste of staff work. *Sociability* was in full swing and made for a most enjoyable workplace. In fact, I gained lifelong friendships, a most noteworthy one being with Marcus Grappler. Marcus, the personification of courage and integrity, would many years later play a major role as a use of force expert in the federal trial of the officers charged with the beating Rodney King.

I did not stay long at Public Affairs as I became aware of an opportunity to promote one level up at another division. This new position at Advance Planning Division was as an officer assigned to a team to develop an automated system for deploying personnel. The job itself was rather boring. I sought "escape" via an open position at Juvenile Division. A certain lieutenant friend of mine from Public Affairs had transferred to Juvenile Division, and through this previous *relationship* I had exhibited a requisite degree of competency.

Access to the "escape" route transpired coincidentally with matrimony. That victim of the bank hold-up back in late 1971 was now the bride at our April 1975 wedding. With the transfer to Juvenile Division, though, hope for a honeymoon of any duration longer than a day was dashed with the transfer to Juvenile Division. In a way, it was instructive in that it demonstrated early on in our marital relationship the extent to which the "best interests of the department" could intervene in family life. Down the road there would be shift changes and transfers that could prove problematic for any relationship unprepared for such eventualities. Down the road, her support of not only my endeavors, but the department's as well, would be formally recognized.

In April 2, 1977, Jill became a patient of the maternity ward at Tarzana Medical Center, and the next day, our family had grown by one. Young Matthew had chosen to arrive at 3:33 a.m. A couple months afterward, the juvenile crime prevention program to which I had been assigned became a casualty of sweeping budgetary cuts.

The program was terminated, and I ended up landing a position at the police academy as an in-service training coordinator. I do think I might have had a boost in securing the academy position because while at Public Affairs I had gained the acquaintance of an individual who was now at the academy. A prior *relationship* came to the rescue.

The officer in charge of the academy workplace was hard-charging Lieutenant Lee Wayne, who would prove instrumental in my career advancement down the road. Lee expected top-notch performance, and at the same time did everything possible to assist in obtaining that level of excellence. He was also a devotee to the importance of growth through higher education and actively encouraged those of us working for him who already had baccalaureate degrees to enroll in a graduate program. With Lee's encouragement, I availed myself of the federal government's Law Enforcement Educational Program funding to complete the highly rated graduate program in public administration at the University of Southern California.

Fast forward to 1980, I was promoted to the position of sergeant. This meant returning to patrol as a field supervisor in West Los Angeles Area. While at West LA in 1982, we paid another visit to the maternity ward for the arrival of our second child, Mollye. Around the same time, I had the good fortune of receiving a doctoral fellowship to Claremont Graduate University; an opportunity I had learned about in the course of habitual *vigilance* accorded the department's monthly consolidated training bulletin. Thus, these family developments prompted the need to increase income.

I successfully interviewed for an advance paygrade sergeant position at Information Resources Division. The stint back in 1974 working on the ADAM project at Advance Planning Division had provided some experience working on automated systems development, and came in handy here when I needed it for a competitive edge. The position required that I prepare a requirements document for a traffic information system. While I was working on wrapping up the traffic system requirements documentation, "Lieutenant Lee," for whom I had worked for at the academy, had promoted a couple ranks and was now in my chain of command. Also, around this time I had noticed an opening for an advanced paygrade sergeant position at Tactical Planning Section. This tactical planning employment opportunity represented a dream job to me. I applied for the planning position, but realized that it could be tough sledding to obtain approval to move to the spot even if selected. The Information Resources Division was attempting to hang onto its cadre of supervisors, fearing that vacancies might not get filled given existing budgetary matters. As it turned out, I was selected for the position, and I believe that Lee must have been the person responsible for cutting the ties that could have held me from transferring. One cannot underestimate the value of *relationship-building*.

Subsequently, Lee requested my presence to serve as his aide in his new position as assistant commanding officer of West Bureau (oversight authority for four patrol divisions and a traffic division). Soon thereafter he was selected for a chief of police position at another southern California police department.

Because aide positions were limited to two-year terms and I was nearing completion of two years, I needed to find another position. I had heard of a task force that was being formed to do a makeover of the department's property and evidence processes. Commander Len Manihatz was in charge of the task force. I had known Len 15 years earlier when I was a member of the National Advisory Commission task force and working for Chad. Len had also been a member of the task force. As it turned out, I met the criteria for the position, and I soon became the project manager of what was referred to as the Automated Property Management System task force (APMS for short). Put another plus in the column for the value of *relationships* and "track record."

In mid-1992, soon after the Los Angeles riots ended, I was promoted to lieutenant. Speaking of the "lieutenancy," I would be remiss to not mention some extraordinary synchronicity that visited around the time I was prepping for the lieutenant's written and oral exams. I was light on policing tactical experience, so one of my "rabbis" (a slang term for an individual of a higher rank supportive of another's promotional worth) inquired as to whether I had any prior military service and its nature. Upon mentioning I had infantry experience in Vietnam, he suggested that I get in touch with a certain individual who had flown helicopters in Vietnam. Perhaps this individual could suggest how the military experience could be integrated with policing to bolster my tactical dimension. I sought out the individual, Lieutenant Norm Rotor, who at the time, coincidentally, was assigned to a position one floor above my base of operations at Parker Center. Upon entering the veteran's office, I noticed on Norm's wall pictures of the same type helicopter I had intimate familiarity with in Vietnam. I volunteered to Norm, "Oh, you flew 'loaches?' One of those choppers opened up on our infantry company one day in May 1970." This piqued his curiosity and he asked for details. As I began to provide details, Norm picked up the story and completed the narrative. As it turned out, he was the pilot of that same helicopter that mistakenly opened fire on our unit! He knew every detail, e.g., type of injuries sustained and the time and location of the incident. To his defense, I learned from Norm that he had been told by another officer aboard the helicopter that supposedly there were no "friendlies" working where we were.

    I turned over the reins of the APMS project to my brilliant assistant, Jack Palace, and headed off to Northeast Area as a patrol watch commander. A note is in order here regarding Jack. Without his presence in the project, the automated portion of the enterprise would not have gotten off the ground. And, too, the work relationship grew to a friendship over the years that extended to his wife, Katie, a psychotherapist. Through the years, Katie was a valuable resource in areas related to stress management and work-family balance. Once again, *relationship-building* proved fruitful.

    I was only at Northeast Area for a few months before being reassigned to Devonshire Area, in the Valley, as the patrol watch commander. Working at Devonshire proved fortuitous as on January 17, 1994, I would have an opportunity to test the effectiveness of the aerial damage assessment plan we had created at Tactical Planning Section back in the mid-'80s. This exercise of planning *initiative* proved pivotal in rapid response to key vital points within the division when at 4:31 a.m. on January 17 the Northridge earthquake struck. This was one of the most powerful and destructive earthquakes to strike California, and its epicenter was in the middle of Devonshire Area. Compounding matters, our family's residence was in Northridge; thus, I was in the less-than-envious position of earthquake victim and first responder. After a few weeks of 12-hour shifts, six days a week, the department returned to normal operations.

In March 1994 I learned that an application submitted to Penn State University to join the criminal justice faculty had been reviewed favorably. I had completed my doctoral studies six years earlier, with the intention of some day teaching full-time. *Initiative* and *perseverance* had yielded a significant dividend. In mid-April I submitted my retirement paperwork to the LAPD.

I must say the transition to university teaching was done with a significant amount of effort—and luck. It had required logging a lot of hours gaining teaching experience at local universities, and that teaching had to dovetail with my police department shifts. In addition, the subjects available to adjuncts were often those which were the least desirable to full-time faculty. Too, the ability to interview for positions at universities throughout the country required juggling of days off to accommodate minimal two-day campus visits. I interviewed at 13 universities, none of them in California. It was not unusual to have gotten off a flight into Los Angeles from North Carolina, Pennsylvania, or other points east two hours before having to preside over start of a watch back in the San Fernando Valley. On a number of occasions, there was a lot of nervous time hoping the weather would hold long enough to get back into the Valley on time (the interviewing occurred between January and March). *Energy* and *resourcefulness* proved to be important sustaining qualities.

Off to "Linebacker U"—Penn State

In August, Jill, Matt, Mollye, and I packed up a rental truck with all our belongings and headed for Pennsylvania. Matt drove my Toyota Camry—which did not have functioning air conditioning—all the way across Interstate 40 (dotted with deserts for many miles at the outset). Also, the Camry was a standard transmission (a rare four-wheel drive sedan), and Matt did a yeoman's job of adapting from his sole previous experience limited to automatic transmissions. Kudos to Matt for his *adaptability*! I drove the truck, and Jill drove our Mercury (with air conditioning).

I assumed my position as an assistant professor at the university's campus at the state capital in Harrisburg, within the School of Public Affairs. It was a new beginning in all ways. I did feel the experience was predestined—despite frequent thoughts about all we had left in California. Here we were now living in an apartment in rural Pennsylvania, after having struggled for years to have finally made it to a nice home in southern California. Things did improve on the residential front; in January during the semester break we relocated to another nicer and more spacious apartment.

I had gotten into the swing of things, blending my practitioner experience with academic research and fashioning lesson plans based on both realms. I had a very capable graduate assistant, Bernice Multaski, who was quite helpful in assisting with the research agenda and covering a class or two when circumstances required my being off campus. Down the road, Bernice was instrumental in my co-authorship of a leading criminal justice textbook. Too, of note, I was able to capitalize on my emergency management experience and the richness of the local environment to craft a unique emergency management course.

A few years into the Penn State experience, Jill's mother's (Rhoda Beam) suffered episodes of a rare form of pustular psoriasis that had worsened to the point of being life-threatening. In addition, we had never been able to sell our home in California at our asking price because home values had plummeted after the earthquake. Instead of selling, it was on the rental market. The tax rule in effect at the time was that the home would lose its status as a privately owned residence if the homeowner did not reside in it two of the most recent five years. Therefore, given Rhoda's chronic illness and the looming tax implications for our unsold home in California, it became essential that Jill return to California to reoccupy our home and to be in close proximity to her mother. This *priority* reigned supreme. Thus, once again we rented a truck and packed it with our household belongings and relocated Jill and Mollye back to our unsold home in California.

I promised Jill I would attempt to find work back in California, and thus I embarked on a campaign to find a job while at the same time wrapping up the loose ends in my quest for tenure (tenure at PSU would in many instances be transferable elsewhere). I made a dozen or so trips to California for job interviews at universities, police departments, emergency management facilities, and the Department of Justice. Here again, just as was the situation in getting to Pennsylvania and a university position, I had to get past some significant logistical challenges to travel cross-country at times convenient for both interviews and my teaching schedule. Too, I had to sandwich in preparation of customized letters and questionnaire responses to potential employers between research publication documents.

In October 1999 *perseverance* paid off as I was offered a position with the California Department of Justice. I must admit that I was fortunate to have known an individual of impeccable integrity, Adam Post, already at DOJ, as this *relationship* likely assisted in my getting a favorable review there. The only downside was that there was little flexibility with the start date. I needed to start no later than the beginning of January 2000, which meant the tenure process would need to be aborted. This was a disappointment in that for five years I had worked until the wee hours of many mornings putting the finishing touches on publication after publication. All the tenure hoops had been jumped through. Having tenure would be an insurance policy of sorts in that if things did not work out at DOJ I would be in a much better position to land a full-time teaching position at a Cal State campus. Nevertheless, the *priority* of returning to California outweighed gaining tenure and remaining in Pennsylvania.

Back to the "Left Coast"

It was time again to rent a truck and a car trailer for a cross-country trek. I reported into my new workplace on January 3, 2000. I was informed my primary responsibility would be to create an instructor certification process and training course for the hundreds of law enforcement instructors in the state. As it turned out, I had the good fortune of having a veteran instructional designer, Dennis Adams, within the same section I was assigned to at DOJ, who answered any questions I had regarding instructional design, learning objectives, and levels of human cognition. After countless meetings with subject matter experts, an academy instructor certification program was rolled out, and the certification process for the hundreds of instructors was underway.

My oversight involvement in the instructional realm rekindled my interest in the classroom experience, and I subsequently became an adjunct faculty member at a couple state university campuses. I found the academic freedom and student interaction to be buoying, contrasting with the rather lock-step, bureaucratic milieu within which I was immersed daily. Students such as Davie Goodfellow, Nicole commfound, and Kevin Nuground exemplified dedication to strengthening communities and improving the quality of life for all residents. Davie and Nicole both attained influential positions in community affairs: Davie as a law enforcement professional and Nicole as a philanthropic coordinator for a prominent northern California community foundation. Kevin went on to earn a master's degree at Arizona State University and pursued a Ph.D. at Washington State University. Kevin was a first generation college student and had defied all odds in barely getting through high school due to extreme childhood challenges.

Also, along with the return to the classroom came an important reconnection with my graduate assistant from Penn State, Bernice. Bernice had secured a professorship with a Cal State campus and recommended me as a potential member of a multi-author team for a budding criminal justice textbook. Through this *networking* I had the good fortune of joining a book authorship team, led by Ruth Worth, that would ultimately produce four editions of a leading textbook. And, moreover, this initial networking led to partnering with the lead author in editing a three-volume criminal justice encyclopedia distributed throughout the United States academic community.

As the instructor program took flight, I was able to move into the arena of detective training as program manager of the state's criminal investigation institute. The institute provided advanced investigative instruction in areas such as computer crime, identity theft, and human trafficking. A key to enhancement of the institute's offerings came in the form of a highly foresightful instructional designer, Steve August. Steve, who was loaned from another unit, employed, his technological acumen in ways that greatly expanded the range of investigative tools available to the state's detective corps. On behalf of Steve, I would offer this as an exceptional example of commitment to *service*.

After about seven years, I was promoted to a bureau chief position. In my case I remained in the bureau already assigned, which included development of legislatively mandated training programs, on-line and video productions, firearms and driving simulators, and Violence Against Women Act (VAWA) grant-funded programs. We experienced a wrinkle with the VAWA grants when an unanticipated loss of the program administrator occurred. Fortuitously, a highly talented and foresightful colleague, Brian Sharp, had recently contracted for a project facilitator to plug any gaps in productivity as the need arose. The person recruited for the position, Denise Davis, proved to be a quick study as she was able to readily assume the complex grant administrator duties as well as assume other time-sensitive responsibilities of the departed individual.

In 2013 I retired from DOJ, completing a career in criminal justice that spanned 42 years. In looking back, there were lots of contributions to the field that bore my fingerprints—alongside those of countless others. Undeniably, law enforcement is a team enterprise. Not only was I able to partner with some exceptional individuals, but I had the good fortune of gaining the trust of people who made hiring decisions. If it were not for those who afforded opportunities to perform, I would never have gotten out of the "starting blocks." Thus, I am huge on taking chances on people and doing all I can to aid in their development and support in the workplace.

Of course, it cannot be emphasized enough the degree to which one's family—immediate and extended— and close friends serve as the bedrock upon which a livelihood is built. Support is crucial. In particular, my brother, Pat, and sister-in-law, Leigh, have been extraordinarily supportive and generous throughout the journey.

My wife and I have moved 12 times. This can cause a strain. However, we always mutually supported each other in the course of the moves. Oftentimes, the moves were necessary to raise funds for continuing our children's education. We pulled equity from each re-sale of our primary residence. It did increase each mortgage, however. This was not a problem, though, in light of the end goal. Our kids never complained about the moves. Speaking of our "kids"—Matt is now 41 and Mollye 36—their extraordinary accomplishments were and have been an ongoing source of pride. Our son heads his own law firm, and Mollye is an accomplished educator and mother of three children.

An Afterthought about Sustaining Qualities

The qualities (e.g., adaptability, relationship-building, etc.) that I have identified as prominent in my life course may be seen to varying degrees in those evidence-based life path determinants cited within the "Research Review." However, one certainly cannot dismiss the possibility of contribution of forces or influences unverifiable by conventional scientific methods. I must say that I have witnessed some uncanny displays of coincidence, or synchronicity as described by Carl Jung. For example, there was my incidental referral from Len to meet with Norm at LAPD headquarters more than two decades after our anonymous "encounter" in Vietnam. Another Vietnam-related meaningful coincidence directly led to publication of this manuscript. I had met up with Doug Dollar, who at the time I was in Vietnam was a junior officer in the same infantry company before transfering to the battalion tactical operations center (and later a major general), at a 2017 reunion of Charlie Company in St. Louis. I came to learn that Doug was in the publishing business and was enthusiastic about the idea of two old Charlie Company grunts helping the younger generation, and others, better understand life's journey.

Moreover, equally compelling, there have been at least three instances where I could not account, at least within the earthly realm, for best case outcomes. The solo cross-country flight in perilous weather was aided by clouds never actually reaching to the ground and thus obscuring totally the land beneath. I often thought the path of the bullet that miraculously missed my jugular vein was deflected by the heavenly hand of my recently deceased father. And, too, somehow the windshield in my upside down Volkswagen popped out with such ease as to trigger recurrent pondering, "How did that materialize?" For lack of plausible material explanation, I heartily opt to attribute these events' outcomes to divine intervention. From my perspective, this translates, in terms of qualities, to *religiousness* and *spirituality*. Religion and spirituality are intertwined. Spirituality is a subjective experience of a sacred dimension, inclusive of the deepest values and meanings by which an individual lives. Religion implies participation in a specific communal practice of divine belief and worship.

Obviously, the sustaining qualities identified by me may be unique to my journey. In Chapter 4, we look at a comprehensive listing of qualities submitted by a number of the individuals ("bumpers") who were impactful in the course of my life path. Through, this compilation, there can be derived sustaining qualities across a range of individuals. Through a content analysis process, qualities common to a majority of individuals are distilled.

Chapter 4

Respondents' Selections of Sustaining Qualities

In recounting my life journey, just "south" of three dozen individuals have been identified as impactful to varying degrees. Twenty of them submitted narratives identifying qualities they believed significant in their own journeys. Others, while not preparing self-reports, endorsed the viability of the case study methodology being employed to mine key sustaining qualities. For example, Chad earnestly advocated using vignettes from significant others' life experiences to show how certain qualities are recurrently recognized as sustaining and how readers may bring key qualities into their lives. Joan enthusiastically supported life reflections, which she believed would be very helpful to people contemplating the next steps in their lives, no matter when they occur.

Before discussing qualities per se, it is essential the composition of the respondent population be described. This enables generalizing findings beyond the study's participants; although, in qualitative research, such as this study, most often the goal is to provide a rich, contextualized understanding of some aspect of the human experience (Polit & Beck, 2010). This case study approach by its nature yielded a small sample size. However, the 20 respondents (plus the author) did encompass representation from diverse demographic sectors: young adults, middle-aged adults, and seniors;

Caucasians, African Americans, Hispanics, and Asians; and female and male genders. Backgrounds range the gamut, which may be gleaned from snippets of life experiences that have been integrated into illustrations of specific qualities' context.

Qualities Identified by Respondents

The qualities enumerated by respondents were couched within their respective narratives' contexts. The qualities were analyzed and melded into eight categories (see Table 4.1). The categories and their composition, along with contextual examples, are presented in order of their significance.

Adaptability. "Adaptability" and its related elements of "openness," "amenability," and "practicality" were pre-eminent among all categories of qualities. This category constituted 21 percent of the aggregate attributes deemed important for sustaining one along a life path. Adaptability was the most common thread for weaving a tapestry of success.

Nicole, one of the three recent college graduates (along with Davie and Kevin) in the study, expressed adaptability's indomitable essence in her candid assessment that early on in the workplace she recognized that the world would not change to accommodate her. She adopted an open mindset that markedly expanded her job prospects and eventually secured a richly satisfying position within the hub of a philanthropic foundation that has benefitted countless individuals and families.

Davie, like Nicole, quickly figured out it was critical to be open to new opportunities. He had been comfortable as a service coordinator at a drive-thru oil change facility, but warmed quickly to a new position in security operations offering a significant benefit package.

Kevin, whose father dropped out of school in the 10th grade and who subsequently was imprisoned in his early 20s, reasoned that if he were to break the cycle of drugs and violence that permeated his life through parental deficits he would have to undertake the transformative actions that would lead him from a dismal academic

Table 4.1

Categories of Qualities in Frequency and as a Percentage of Impactful Others' Selections

Quality and Sub-Elements	Frequency	Percentage of Responses

Adaptability
  Openness
  Amenability
  Practicality
	24	21

Perseverance
  Resiliency
  Industrious
  Focus
	18	15

Relationship-Building
  Collaborative
  Communicative
	16	14

Supportive
  Loyal
  Respectful
  Loving
	15	13

Self-Improvement Pro-Mentoring	13	11

Initiative
  Resourceful
  Vigilant (for opportunities)
	11	9

Value-Driven Optimistic	11	9
Service Orientation Caring	9	8

Note: "Frequency" is representative of responses from 20 individuals, plus the author. Responses were organized into eight primary categories and analogous sub-elements. Thus, for example, respondents' selections of "resiliency," "industrious", and "focus" were subsumed within the category of "perseverance," which altogether totaled 18. Literally, "perseverance" was chosen 8 times, "resilience" was chosen 4 times, "industrious" 5 times, and "focus" once (totaling 18).

background to college graduation. He ultimately did graduate from continuation high school (after failing the majority of high school classes) and is now a doctoral candidate at a major university in the Pacific Northwest. His path was made possible through balancing a succession of part-time jobs with academic schedules.

Brian expressed that he experienced many highly impactful junctures, and he often found it best to just "go with it." He added that something that has gotten him through a number of life challenges has been knowing when to move on; redirection may often be the best strategy.

Len became a policing executive and later a top-level aviation safety administrator for the federal government. He offered that he originally worked as a police officer to support his education and attend law school. Once in the law enforcement door, though, he realized it was the right career for him. Thus he changed his course of travel through life to include a career in policing. Similarly, at various junctures in his career he was tasked with duties that were foreign to him in concept and downright mystifying. One such duty was automating the police department's property management system, another one was developing the agency's business plan for automated systems. In hindsight he recognized that had he not been flexible and open to new challenges, he might have wasted his time complaining rather than embracing the challenges and learning from them.

My sister-in-law, Bev, is a social worker and an attorney. She contributes bountiful energy to problem-solving on behalf of the homeless. In the course of her efforts, her watchword has been openness. She has evinced receptivity to the realities and constraints of the situation, but at the same time has been demonstrably adaptable in considering for implementation the spectrum of remedies from all quarters.

Perseverance. "Perseverance" enveloped "industrious" and "resilience." It constituted 15 percent of respondents' choices.

Katie saw and integrated the value of hard work at the early age of 13, working weekends at an aunt's real estate office. From that time forward she always had a part-time job: childcare, waitressing, summer playground director, cleaning houses, etc. Her parents were both of Mexican heritage and had experienced ridicule growing up in U.S. border towns, with Spanish being their first language. Her parents' decision to not teach her and her siblings Spanish had a lasting impact on her. It created cognitive dissonance in regard to her developing a sense of identity. By the time she decided to learn Spanish in college, it was a huge challenge. However, this perseverance became for her one of the most enduring qualities and a major factor in her ability to effectively respond to the challenges she has encountered throughout her career as a psychotherapist.

Lee's work ethic and resilience were rooted in his upbringing in a small mining town. Neither of his parents got to high school, and his father did not complete grammar school before he and his two brothers ran away from home. The lack of education on the part of both parents influenced him negatively. He did not know what or how to study. He barely made it through high school. A close friend talked him into getting into law enforcement. After becoming a member of the force, he found himself struggling with reports, communications, and personal discipline. He subsequently enrolled in several English grammar classes and studied vocabulary earnestly. He eventually recognized through observing the practices of others who were promoted that the path to upward mobility was paved with hard work and self-discipline. This inspired him to further his formal education, which he did, culminating in a graduate degree in public administration from one of the nation's top universities. Ultimately, Lee rose to a high staff officer position within the agency, followed a few years later with appointment to the chief executive officer position with a major southern California police department. Interestingly, while serving as chief of police, he was selected by Harvard University to serve on its distinguished panel of police leaders overseeing creation of the *Perspectives on Policing* series of reports (Kelling, 1988). The reports became a foundation for police executive training across the nation.

Rocky faced an uphill battle early on. His parents were frequently incarcerated and as a result he was frequently made a ward of the court. This led to institutional confinement for substantial portions of his youth. Throughout the period he also lost family members to gun violence. As a 19-year-old, he was drafted into the U.S. Army and trained as a medic. He was twice wounded in Vietnam in service as a combat medic. In hindsight, he feels that his ability to survive the rising tide of stress, trauma, and tragedy was owed in large part to the steadfast character of his grandfather. His grandfather was the sole reliable figure in his life and was the one individual who could be consistently relied on to fill the parental void in his life. The determination he saw in his grandfather to make whatever sacrifices were necessary to bring stability to young Rocky's life left an indelible imprint on his psyche: *"resilience and determination = success against all odds."*

My brother, Pat, is an attorney. When responding to my question about prominent sustaining qualities, he without hesitation answered "resiliency." The name of the game for him has always been bouncing back from adversity, and the chief means for rebounding consistently been "nose to the grindstone." Adversity ranged from having to overcome injuries suffered in sports to having to be one of the handful of law school students who had to work to support himself while immersed full-time in highly demanding course work. While a very successful litigator, he did experience those "do or die" moments "against the ropes," but always maintained the necessary fortitude to carry on.

Relationship-Building. "Relationship-building," inclusive of "collaborative" and "communicative," followed closely behind "perseverance." "Relationship-building" comprised 14 percent of the selections.

Steve could be considered a "poster person" for the value of relationship-building. It has proven to be part and parcel of his journey. He is currently in his fourth industry since starting his career as a performance consultant. He started in the high tech world in

Silicon Valley, moved to law enforcement, transitioned to retail, and shifted gears to the automotive sector. Building relationships was the most important activity in learning, growing, and understanding each industry. For example, upon immersion into the Silicon Valley milieu, Steve made it a priority to learn the interests of his co-workers. He learned that many were surfers and spent the morning in the surf before coming to work. He would thus begin conversations with them by asking, "How were the waves this morning?" By simply asking a question about something they were interested in, he changed the dynamic between them. As he spent more time with them in this vein, work conversations evolved from formal meetings on the calendar to organic discussions that got to the underlying issues. The occasional "pop-in" to ask a work question was met with less and less resistance. Over time there was mutual appreciation for the contributions each made to the workplace.

Bernice is a devotee to the premise that it is really important to have someone who believes in you and who is willing to help navigate the journey. She cautions, though, while it is invaluable to have someone influential who believes in you, it is essential that individual be in a position to help. Otherwise, they cannot contribute to propelling you to the next level. If the "planets do align" and a relationship results in an opportunity, promptly expressing appreciation for supportive others' time and effort is essential. Of course, any effort by another on one's behalf, regardless of whether or not it leads to an opportunity, is deserving of grateful acknowledgement.

Ruth valued very much having positive relationships personally and professionally. When given management responsibilities she quickly realized she was not an authoritarian leader; rather, she was "a steward of my colleagues, or first among equals in my leadership position." She valued compromising with others, which often proved to be the optimal outcome among other options. Accordingly, she was amenable to giving others the time to fully express their thoughts on matters.

Supportive. The category of "supportive" was comprised of "loyalty," "respectful," and "loving." The category garnered 13 percent of respondents' choices. "Supportiveness" was expressed in a dual context. While many responses to identification of sustaining qualities were oriented toward achieving successful outcomes in the workplace, when "supportiveness" was nominated as a prominent sustaining quality it often was cited as emanating outside the workplace.

The leading quality listed by Len in his narrative was the importance of a supportive and strong spouse. His wife put up with odd hours, weekend duty, many holidays worked, and the overall stress of his law enforcement career. Her support ranged from mere tolerance to actually getting involved as a volunteer in community initiatives where Len worked. "Along the way she gave lots and lots of advice and counsel."

Dennis related that his wife, after his parents, was the most influential person in his life. She taught him much about service, writing, and learning. They were constantly collaborating on their various individual projects. Dennis credits his hardworking father, a baker, as the model for the work ethic that enabled him to forge on. His mother emphasized the importance of education and was helpful and supportive throughout his schooling (which later proved foundational for his success in doctoral studies).

Brian offered that connecting with his wife was key to any success he has attained in the workplace. Their relationship has been one of mutual supportiveness, both in the course of job changes and geographic relocations.

As previously alluded to in the discussion of relationship-building, Bernice wholeheartedly endorsed the value to be derived from having a "sponsor" in the workplace. "Having someone who believes in you and who is willing to help navigate the tough things or to put you in positions where you can really lead and succeed is a true blessing."

Art held a critically responsible position while serving as an infantry commanding officer. He valued loyalty a great deal. As someone close to him "24-7" (as his radio man), I witnessed the extent to which he demonstrated loyalty to country and to the mission at hand. And he was equally loyal to the men of his command. Their welfare was of paramount importance. He respected opinions from all quarters. He spent as much time listening and consulting with non-commissioned personnel as he did with commissioned officers. He had a company largely comprised of conscripts who would have very much preferred to be anywhere else on the planet. Had his soldiers not felt his support, the perilous work to be done could not have been accomplished.

Self-Improvement. "Self-improvement" included seeking and enlisting a mentor. The category comprised 11 percent of the qualities cited. I was somewhat surprised with the extent to which a zeal for self-improvement was present in the backgrounds of the respondents.

It was gratifying to see that the four youngest respondents (Davie, Nicole, Denise, and Kevin) had all accorded mentoring as instrumental in getting to where they find themselves today. At the same time, it was reassuring to see senior respondents (e.g., Ruth, Len, and Lee) expressing appreciation for the value of role models, mentoring, and education in their respective ascents to executive positions.

Pat Gallup had come from a large family (eleven members) with little structure in early life for success. He had low self-esteem and seemingly poor academic acumen. In fact, he had been held back twice in the third grade. A 1.9 GPA in high school was not promising for a rosy future. In early adulthood, it was discovered he suffered from attention deficit hyperactivity disorder. Eventually, a combination of self-starting goals, great track coaches, and insightful teachers enabled qualities that had been dormant to shine through. He gained the confidence to not hold back in communicating and to assume leadership roles in many facets of his life. Pat became adept at "identifying my fears in others and leading them from 'blind alleys', pointing them in the direction of achievable goals."

Pat evolved to become an alternate on a USA Olympics track team delegation and a meritorious law enforcement supervisor.

Initiative. "Initiative" included "resourcefulness" and "vigilance" (the state of being watchful for opportunities). It accounted for nine percent of the aggregate.

Brian very much personified the essence of "initiative." He seemed to practice initiative naturally. The positions he has held in government agencies have all been of the coveted variety. Just as the hiring entities put forth maximum efforts in finding the right person for filling their demanding positions, Brian, in turn, did his "homework" in identifying upcoming openings and positions for which he would be competitive. As importantly, he prepared extremely well for the interview process. Interestingly, too, he was proactive in recognizing when it was time to move on to other opportunities. This heightened his vigilance in watching for junctures that would lead to next stops in his professional development. In the course of his various positions, he astutely availed himself of opportunities that would further enhance his capabilities and qualifications. In the course of his employment in law enforcement, he gained admittance to the prestigious FBI National Academy program. And too, while working in state government, he was able to earn a doctorate degree, which added significantly to his portfolio.

Denise resembled Brian in terms of her degree of initiative. In fact, Brian was the person who hired her as a project facilitator when he was working in state government. Denise was and has been constantly vigilant for positions that would allow her to grow. After leaving her contracted position in state government, she quickly landed positions of ever-increasing responsibility within the educational environment. She is currently enrolled in a doctoral program, with graduation on the foreseeable horizon. Denise's responses to sustaining quality prioritization reflected the qualities that drive "initiative": determination, focus, self-motivation, and self-improvement.

Rocky has demonstrated initiative through his efforts to emulate his late grandfather's dedication and compassion. He has assumed a significant measure of responsibility of caretaker for his two nieces, following the incarceration of their father. He has made it a point to be part of their lives and to let them know they are loved and special.

Value-Driven. Implicit in this category of "value-driven" is one's alignment with standards of behavior. It includes the inclination to put the most favorable construction upon actions or to anticipate the best possible outcome, i.e., "optimism." "Value-driven" constituted the same percentage of the total qualities as "initiative," i.e., nine percent. While not as frequently cited as being a prominent quality to the extent "adaptability" and "perseverance" and some others were, it's my belief that "value-driven" may not have been readily discernible as a separable, discrete concept. In any case, there was a special richness to the narratives that singled out adherence to values as an essential quality.

In her youth, Ruth had been set on a career as an astronomer. She changed her career orientation numerous times, finally settling on the social sciences. A key factor that led her to the social sciences was her immersion in the 1960s atmosphere while attending the University of California at Berkeley. She became a devotee to "speaking truth to power." She was loyal to this dictum throughout her career as a parole officer and subsequent role as the department chairperson of the criminology department at a major California university. Indeed, Ruth was quick to bring to my attention the potential value of James Comey's 2018 book, *A Higher Loyalty: Truth Lies, and Leadership*, for use in a course on ethical leadership. Mr. Comey was renown for his stance that ethical leaders speak the truth and know that making wise decisions requires people to tell them the truth.

Another individual who has "walked the talk' of best ethical practices is Marcus. He was faced with an extraordinary test of character when he was asked to testify on the use of force employed by the Los Angeles police officers in the infamous Rodney King beating incident. At the time, Marcus was an LAPD Academy instructor teaching use of force tactics and practices. At the federal civil rights trial of two LAPD officers facing imprisonment for alleged excessive force, Marcus testified that as a subject matter expert he could not justify the extent of force used against King. While an extraordinarily stressful experience, Marcus remained true to the highest values espoused by both the law enforcement code of ethics and his own moral compass.

Len volunteered simple and powerful advice he received from a key mentor. When confronted with difficult management challenges, he was told that he should find the correct underlying principle and decision making and problem solving would become markedly easier.

Jill placed "morals " at the top of her list of sustaining qualities. The selection was qualified to include a requisite degree of conviction and a loving and optimistic outlook, and the tenacity to safely navigate the "high road" amid stretches where "guard rails" may be lacking.

Service Orientation. The desire to be of service to others was the eighth of the eight categories of sustaining qualities. It followed by one percentage point the categories of "initiative" and "value-driven."

At this juncture, it is instructive to recollect Rocky's dedication to service. While not volunteering for military service, once conscripted his dedication to serving his brother infantrymen as a combat medic was exemplary.

While Rocky's commitment to service surfaced while in a capacity for which he had not originally volunteered, Dennis is an individual who has actively chosen the service path when presented with an array of opportunities. Following college graduation in the mid-1960s he joined the Peace Corps. He was sent to Afghanistan where he taught English as a foreign language in Afghan schools. Following his Peace Corps service, he pursued a graduate degree in education at the American University of Beirut. He subsequently earned a doctorate in educational technology and spent decades in education-related service to numerous governmental and private-sector organizations. Upon his retirement, he took a position with "BloodSource" as a driver delivering and picking up blood. On the side, he researched, developed, and presented illustrated programs on Islam and the Middle East.

While being one of four male siblings and raised primarily by my father, I have been most fortunate to have had extraordinary sisters-in-law, and to have received from each of them timely and caring support. Too, I have observed each of them provide loving support to others. In this regard, Leigh has personified caring for others to the "nth" degree. She has been a crusader for the welfare of aged individuals who find themselves residing in senior care facilities. She has made substantial donations of goods (e.g., shoes) to those without. Her degree of care for and service to others encompasses the widest spectrum of individuals, from those representing formal charities to day laborers encountered at random.

Qualities Identified by Students

All the qualities identified to this point have been those of comparatively experienced life path travelers. In order to ascertain the value of their pronouncements, it is necessary to contrast their selections with the mindsets of those embarking on their life journeys. This has been accomplished by surveying students enrolled in a criminal justice policy class at a northern California university campus. The 44 students enrolled in the fall 2018 class were requested to cite qualities they believed would be instrumental in fulfilling their aspirations. Class level breakdown was 20 freshmen, 11 sophomores, 9 juniors, and 4 seniors. Breakdown by major was as follows: 13 undeclared, 13 criminal justice, 11 social sciences, and 7 physical sciences. Gender breakdown was 24 females and 20 males. All the students could be viewed as "traditional" in their composition by age (late teens and early twenties).

The qualities identified by students were analyzed and, as was the case with the experienced individuals, were categorized into eight clusters (see Table 4.2). However, experiential narratives were not requested from the students, given their youthfulness.

After comparing the responses of the two disparate groups, i.e., the 44 inexperienced students against the 21 life-experienced individuals, significant differences were readily observable. With the students, intrinsic qualities were emphasized. Motivation was at the top of the list, followed by perseverance, endowed characteristics such as patience mental toughness, perceived workplace skillset, and knowledge. Sociability and vigilance (for opportunities) were at the bottom, and decidedly so, accounting for only nine percent of responses. The experienced group, on the other hand, appeared far more attuned to extrinsic factors such as adaptability and relationship-building.

Table 4.2

Categories of Qualities in Frequency and as a Percentage of Student's Selections

Quality and Sub-Elements	Frequency	Percentage of Responses

Motivation
    Drive
    Determination
    Commitment
	32	24

Perseverance
    Resiliency
    Industrious
    Focus
	29	22

Endowed Characteristics
    Mental Toughness
    Physically fit
    Patient
    Creative
	20	15

Refined Workplace Skills
    Problem Solver
    Thorough
    Punctual
    Time Management Acumen
	17	13

Knowledgeable
    Educated
    Critical Thinker
	12	9

Value-Driven
    Optimistic
    Integrity
    Honesty
    Just
	11	8

Sociability
    Personable
    Relationship-Building
    Community Engaged
	10	8

Continued on next page.

| Vigilant Opportunistic | 2 | 1 |

Note: "Frequency" is representative of responses from 44 students. Responses were organized into eight primary categories and analogous sub-elements. Thus, for example, respondents' selections of "resiliency," "industrious", and "focus" were subsumed within the category of "perseverance," which altogether totaled 29. In turn, the category of "perseverance" constituted 22 percent of responses.

Chapter 5
Epilogue

The time line upon which my own journey has been traced, as well as that of those who have been of significant influence, obviously is of a previous era. However, the individuals who provided narratives with key qualities did range the gamut age-wise. There was representation from those who came of age in the 1960s through those who entered adulthood just a few years ago. There was noticeable similarity in selection of qualities across all ages. Thus it did not seem that much time immersed in society as a self-sufficient individual was needed to gain an appreciation for key sustaining qualities.

What was readily observable was the difference overall in those who had not yet become fully self-sustaining, i.e., the 44 full-time college students comparison group. Given perseverance was a quality appreciated by both students and workplace-experienced respondents, there were for the most part top to bottom differences in the majority of qualities identified. The difference was between intrinsic and extrinsic qualities. Students ranked internal qualities such as motivation, mental toughness, industriousness, and problem-solving acumen high. Conversely, the societally immersed respondents rated "relationship-building," "amenability," and "supportiveness" (of others) as key qualities. Thus it can be surmised until one is immersed in the process of navigating society as a mature member the value of sociability as a key attribute may very well not be fully appreciated. It is through the process of fitting into mainstream society that one gains knowledge of the importance of getting along with others and establishing a "track record."

In today's fast-paced and rapidly changing society, it behooves one entering the societal fray to be as equipped as possible beforehand. Metaphorically, it is rather like merging into freeway traffic—best to be at the same speed as the traffic flow when merging.

Successful, experienced life path travelers constitute a proven brain trust. Tapping into the collective's reservoir of knowledge yields a fast-track preparatory opportunity. This reservoir, distilled from this study's research findings, can be tapped to create a composite of an individual ideally endowed for traversing a life pathway. The qualities are at hand in the listing prepared as Table 4.1.

The sustained qualities are best absorbed when one's mindset is attuned to the reality that life's journey is traveled along a dynamic pathway. Individuals and events continually exert their influence. One has to be at the ready to adjust to the circumstances presented. In some instances, immediate unilateral decision making will yield the best outcome. On other occasions, a scenario might be best treated by careful, extended deliberation, or acquiescence. It is not possible to fully anticipate the contours or intensity of a potential intervening force; the only forgone certainty is that one's pathway will continuously encounter variables posing course-changing potential. Chapter 2, "Research Review," covered in depth the nature of chance encounters, and means for increasing the potential for favorable outcomes. The chapter also examined spirituality, religion, and parapsychology and their place in navigating a life path for individuals receptive to such.

This book has been prepared as a contribution to the next generation up. Personally, as challenging as I found life's path to be, I do believe it was more easily traveled than what the next generation faces. The "greatest generation" did a very good job of paving the way for us "baby boomers." Making a living and attaining middle class status were not nearly as formidable as they appear for those men and women "next up" in the succession of fulfilling "the American dream." Acquiring a house was well within the capabilities of most Americans. Too, an advanced educational level was not as essential as it is today—and not nearly as expensive. Too, the nature of the workplace has gone global. One starting a business years ago had a far better chance of attaining longevity in the marketplace and not being out-competed by the "big-box" complexes dotting today's landscape or by those throngs acquiring their goods online.

Again, the key qualities identified by the 21 individuals in their narratives represent a collection representative of a large portion of the U.S. population. These key qualities are timeless. Adaptability is as important, or even more so, today, given the rate of change. And perseverance continues to be the tie-breaker when it comes to succeeding in the marketplace. Moreover, relationship-building and collaboration are every bit as critical in the virtual environment. To the extent one is willing to consider application of the qualities to herself or himself, all the better the potential for a fulfilling journey. May the qualities be with you!

References

Adamson, M. (2000). *Does God answer our prayers?* Retrieved from https://www.everystudent.com/wires/prayers.html.

Bandura, A. (1982). The psychology of chance encounters and life paths. *American Psychologist, 8*(7), 747-755.

Carmichael, E. (2016), January 14). Malcolm Gladwell's top 10 rules for success [video file]. Retrieved from https://www.lighthouseofchrist.org/your-field-blog/malcolm-gladwells-top-10-rules-for-success-by-evan-carmichael

Cassidy, G. (2016). *A soldier's story: The Colonel Butch Cassidy memoirs, Volume I*. p. vii. Self-published by Gary N. Cassidy (unknown location).

Cherry, K. (2018, January). 10 Influential psychologists: A look at eminent thinkers in psychology. *Very Well Mind*. Retrieved from https://www.verywellmind.com/most-influentialpsychologists

Clancy, F. (1985, November 14). 'Activists weren't long-haired freaks, but people who saw that some things were wrong and were moved to change them.': Ex-athlete chronicles '60s protests at csun on video. *The Los Angeles Times*. Retrieved from http://articles.latimes.com/1985-11-14/news/vw-2481_1_paul-kulak

Comey, J. (2018). *A higher loyalty: Truth, lies, and leadership*. New York, NY: Flatiron Books.

Dietert, R., & Dietert, J. (2014). *Tools for innovation in science and technology*. Retrieved from http://ebookcentral.proquest.com/

Fritog, A. (2007, November). Keynote Speaker, Honoring all who served. Veterans Day commemoration conducted at the meeting of the Buncombe County Veterans Council, Asheville, North Carolina.

Gladwell, M. (2000). *The tipping point*. New York, NY: Little Brown.

Gross-loh, C. (2016, December). How praise became a consolation prize. *The Atlantic*. Retrieved from https://theatlantic.com/education/archive/2016/12/how-praise-became-a-consolation-prize/510845/

Institute of Noetic Sciences (2018). What are the Noetic Sciences? Retrieved from http://noetic.org/about/what-are-noetic-sciences

Jobs, S. (2005, June 12). Re: Stanford commencement address by steve jobs [Web site video]. Retrieved from https://news.standford.edu/2005/06/14/jobs-061505

Kelling, G.L. (1988) *Police and communities: The quiet revolution* (report No. 1). Boston, MA: Harvard University, John F. Kennedy School of Government.

Mishlove, J. (ed.) (1997). *The roots of consciousness: The classic encyclopedia of consciousness studies revised and expanded*. San Francisco, CA: Council Oak Books.

Peters, M.L., Flink, I.K., Boersma, K., & Linton, S.J. (2010). Manipulating optimism: Can imagining a best possible self be used to increase positive future expectancies? *The Journal of Positive Psychology, 5*(3), 204-211.

Polit, D.F., & Beck, C.T. (2010). Generalization in quantitative and qualitative research: myths and strategies. *International Journal of Nursing Studies, 47*(11), 1451-68.

Radford, B. (2014, February 4). Re: Synchronicity: Definition & meaning (online forum comment). Retrieved from https://www.livescience.com/43105-synchronicity-definition-meaning.html

Rubin, V.L., Burkell, J., & Quan-Haase, A. (2011). Facets of serendipity in everyday chance encounters: A grounded theory approach to blog analysis. *Information Research, 16*(3), 1-21. Retrieved from http://www.informationr.net?ir/16-3/paper488.html

Surprise, K. (2012). *Synchronicity*. Pompton Plains, NJ: Career Press.

Todd, E. (2017). *The infinite view*. New York, NY: Tarcher & Perigee.

Tomasulo, D. (2011). Optimism and the psychology of chance encounters. *Psych Central*. Retrieved from https://psychcentral.com/blog/optimism-and-the-psychology-of-chance-encounters/

Thurston, M. (2017). *Discovering your soul's purpose*. New York, NY: Tarcher & Perigee.

Wiseman, R. (2003, May/June). The luck factor. *Skeptical Inquirer, 27*(3), 1-5.

About the Author

Michael Hooper, Ph.D., is currently a Lecturer in Criminology and Criminal Justice Studies at Sonoma State University. Previously, he served with the California Department of Justice, Penn State University, and Los Angeles Police Department. His most recent publications include co-authorship of the third edition of *CJ: Realities and Challenges* (a textbook published by McGraw-Hill, 2017) and lead editor of the second edition of *Criminal Justice* (a three-volume encyclopedia published by Salem Press in 2017).

Throughout the course of his 40+ years in the criminal justice system as a practitioner and academic (and a stint in the U.S. Army), he observed the gamut of humankind and existences. He had always pondered just how people came to where they ultimately found themselves in life. The desire to actively pursue some degree of an answer to the question came recently while reflecting on students' career ambition cards. He was impressed with the specificity of career aspirations but, at the same time, struck by the realization that, in his experience, unanticipated intersections with people and events would likely intervene to affect life course changes. Thus, this handbook was born from the quest to seek and impart to others the qualities that could prove sustaining amid a life's journey—despite the inevitable twists and turns.

www.ingramcontent.com/pod-product-compliance
Lightning Source LLC
Chambersburg PA
CBHW060503110426
42738CB00055B/2599